A PIECE OF ME

A CONTEMPORARY POETRY COLLECTION

SARAH WILSON

Edited by
ALESHA ESCOBAR
Edited by
AMY PEREZ

DEDICATION

To my husband, my rock...

CONTENTS

ACKNOWLEDGMENTS

For the last sixteen years, I owe much gratitude to my husband David, because he has been my rock, my caretaker, my best friend, and my inspiration.

I also want to thank my best friend Amy who has been my biggest supporter and cheerleader. She always believed in me, and she knows I'm capable of many things, even though it has been hard.

Thanks to my sister Lina for being my confidante and shoulder to cry on, and equally important are my mom and dad, because even from far away they show me their love everyday. And of course, thanks to you Alesha Escobar for helping me make a dream come true. This is the beginning of many new fantasies coming to life on paper for the world.

MONDAY

I remember that Monday,
      as if it were yesterday.
You were on the train, so was I, it was afternoon.
I saw you there, my eyes and yours were one,
I could breathe no longer.

YOUR CRIMSON LIPS CALLED MINE,
    as they looked so soft and tender.
    Those dark eyes looking at me,
    as dark as onyx hidden deep in the earth,
    bright like the moon on a clear night.

MY IMAGINATION RAN WILD,
    as I saw myself making love to you
    under the blackened expanse.
    After that moment, every Monday,
    I look for you on the train.
    But you never appeared again.

WITHOUT VOICE and sense of time, I looked for you,
  with no success my king.
  Each Monday I was there,
  but your face I did not see.
  Please come back and share the view
  with me from the window.

GIVE me life with your smile,
  give me hope with your beautiful eyes
  gazing into mine.
  Monday has only become a day of torture,
  for the train is empty without you,
  a lost destination.
  After that day I lost the possibility of ever
  loving you,
  truly to the end of our journey.

EVERYTHING IS GONE,
  my desire, my voice,
  my soul as the ticking of my heart
  turns into a time bomb ready to explode.
  Why are you not where you should be?

TELL me when you are coming back
  so I can turn back the hands of time,
  to embrace that moment in a timeless cage.
  You are my "angel eyes,"
  the dark eyes that I will patiently
  wait for every Monday and into forever.

IMMORTAL

Today I want to explore all the slopes
and peaks on your body
that lead my hands to wondrous places.
For it is the last time in this virgin forest
and uninhabited land
that we get lost together.

I WANT to transfer all boundaries
of your best-kept corners
to the inner realm
of your secret desires,
where no one has ever been
and never will go,
where not even the hot sun has touched.

I WILL BE the first and the last to enjoy
the sweet treats in your soft skin
inhabited by mortals...

TODAY I WANT to be immortal,
    to remain sunken forever in
    your moist breath,
    entwined with your kisses.
    I want to be the only one
    to glance at your breasts so closely,
    the only one to feel the fever of
    your infinite lust and madness overtake me.

I WILL SECURE my love to ensure that only
    I have the privilege of riding your waist,
    and that my lips have kissed your
    threshold uncontrollable.
    I have all these gifts saved for you, my love,
    one moment replaying over
    and again in my heart and body.
    My heart and body is yours alone, my lover,
    and you can be sure that it belongs
    to you--and only you, until the end.

IMPOSSIBLE

I refuse to believe that love
can be impossible,
when the words are uttered,
they are unheard in my ears.
Two people who find themselves
late in life, with the desire to start
a new chapter that can't be written,
because the story is being told
with someone else.

ALL THE PASSION, love and desire,
are prolonged and yet truncated
by a piece of paper and a golden circle.
It baffles my heart and
deeply saddens my soul,
that I arrived too late.
It is a painful truth, our meeting,
with no remedy.
Why does love have to be impossible

and so out of reach?

YOU BELONG TO HER.
I belong to him.
It was written in a hidden page,
from which I wish to be torn.

A BOOK WITHOUT A HAPPY ENDING,
one where I was not made for you
and you were never mine.
Even though, I finally understand
this bitter truth, that you were
not made for me,
Now the only way I can
console my heart is by dreaming
of you, as if you were in my life.

AND IN SILENCE, I will love you eternally,
always and forever,
my beautiful, secret love.

YOUR TOUCH

When you touch me,
    I feel things that I've never felt;
many sensations that I never
thought I could feel.
All these wonderful emotions that
only my body can feel with your touch.

To RESIST such exquisite feelings would be
    to deny the existence of love.
    When your hands caress my body,
    I know you feel my soul flying to you.

WHEN YOU TOUCH MY ARMS,
    I feel the pores of my skin breathe slowly,
    When our lips touch, I feel the intensity,
    the warmth of your sweet mouth,
    The perfect blend between the sweetness
    of our endless kisses and secret touch.

WHEN YOU LAY your body with mine,
    our skin create a perfect rhythm
    of tender love. As our bodies move
    in unison, they create a song,
    one that we call passion and lust.

YOU ARE capable of touching my heart
    in so many ways, you make me feel the power
    and strength of your love.

MY HEART BEATS, throbbing for you,
    quickly rushing blood through my veins
    like an endless wave.

YOU WERE MADE FOR ME,
    the accurate measurement for my body
    and my heart, no more, no less.

TOUCHING ME, touching you,
    is the most pleasurable feeling,
    I cannot resist.

OUR BODIES WERE MEANT to be as one…
    touching me, touching you.

LONELINESS

*L*oneliness is my best companion
    and my most faithful friend to the end.
    I feel this way often,
but I never speak a word
that belongs to me.

I HONESTLY THINK I'm falling
  in love with my loneliness.

MY HEART IS NOT BEING BROKEN or fractured,
  loneliness is kind and constant,
  She is always there, my sweet confidante,
  no judgment or shame.

THE SHADOW IN MY WINDOW,
  within these walls and each room,

with every step she is there with me.
My dearest loneliness, my confidante,
my partner in crime...
the light that shines through
when my dark days are frequently empty.

YOU ARE ALWAYS THERE, without me calling you,
your tender silence keeps me company.
You breathe on my neck, telling me quietly,
"Tomorrow I will see you again."

MY DEAR LONELINESS, I have no time to miss you,
for you are even in my cold sheets.
In my bed, you are a faithful lover at night,
the friendliest companion in the moonlight.

I WOULD NEVER SAY goodbye to you,
for I am here, even when
the coldest rain falls down on me.
As the wind passes through me,
you surprise me with your warm touch.
Ohhh my dear loneliness,
I thank you for your
constant silence, love.

I WANT you with me forever,
for without you I cannot sleep,
you are the owner of my dreams.
I need you with me, don't ever leave me,

only you understand me.

So STAY, stay with me.
    linger side-by-side,
    and be my eternal
    companion in death.

JUNGLE LOVE

*T*oday I do not want to think,
      nor organize my thoughts.
I do not have a motive,
nor a reason to decide or choose.

I DECIDED NOT to change my ideas,
      or my actions with logic.
      I do not wish to deny this crazy reality.
      I do not want to imagine a perfect world
      and a life eternal.
      I do not wish to think about how far away
      impossible might be.

I JUST KNOW TODAY,
      I want to hold you close to me,
      to feel the warmth of your breath.
      I want to caress your face gently

and kiss you tenderly,
as if you were a child,
so innocent and pure.

I WANT to trail the maps of your body,
with each caress a new sensation.
I wish to make my kiss the only one
your mouth desires and to gently
drink from your navel as if
you were a forbidden fruit.

I WANT to touch your iron legs
so strong and roam around slowly,
as if you were leading me down
a path that leads to your manhood.
I arrive at your ivory tower and revel
in its taste so sweet,
as I crave it over and over.

MY SANITY IS OVERCOME with passion
when I kiss your whole being.
I am drenched from head to toe
as I pine over you, remaining silent,
waiting for your response to my moist jungle,
screaming for its beast to be captured.

I NEED you as I need air to live,
as water to quench my thirst,
like a refreshing rain to cool the

steaming passion that your kisses ignite.

YOUR LOVE IS the source of my life,
    and so my life as it is today,
    I will not think or decide to change ....
    I just want to be... to love you endlessly.

PLEASE DON'T GO

W hy do you have to go,
    stay here with me, stay longer
When you are far, I cannot resist
the loneliness you leave.

STAY A LITTLE LONGER, and give me
    the pleasure of loving you
    Stay and let me revel in your lips of honey.
    You do not know how I feel when
    there is only your shadows.

BECAUSE YOU HAVE to leave me,
    perhaps you do not feel my body
    throb for you. Stay and let me be blend
    with you and see your smile shine
    Do not give me excuses and stay,
    do not put limitations on our hearts
    Why do you have to go?

I MISS your breath and your essence
    I want to explore forever
    the geography of your body.
    Stay and let me adorn your skin
    with rose petals, please don't go,
    I need your sweet smell to survive.
    Stay and let me see the moon
    reflected in your blue eyes.

IN LOVE

When you love someone,
 your heart beats and gives
you away. Your palms become sweaty
with just a skin rub. Your body vibrates
and your blood runs faster.

YOU LOSE the concept of time and days.
 Your mouth is filled with new words
 to describe beauty.
 Your stomach is filled with a
 colorful butterfly forest.

YOUR SMILE BECOMES great and
 shines with his presence
 When you love someone,
 everything is poetry by your side.
 With one kiss you stop breathing
 for a moment. When you love,

everything ceases to exist around you.

THERE'S only room for two,
 you and me together in one
 It's what you make me feel,
 you've always been, and you will be
 My life, my everything, and
 my heart feels complete.

*A*ging is unavoidable,
  it was already written
on the roadmap of life.
Time has no clemency for us,
and is without hesitation or mercy.

OUR BODIES, full of life,
 physical appearance,
 and goals, suddenly change,
 that distant friend, the one who you
 have avoided for some time,
 shows up uninvited.

DOING the impossible to keep it away,
 and in just a moment
 it can overrun your body.
 From head to toe,

an endless weaving, of a beautiful
silver path which covers
your head with no pity.

THOSE BEAUTIFUL SILVER threads
have a long history of joys
and sorrows in between each strand.
In time, jumbled, uneven lines
on your skin appear,
hugging so tightly to your face,
neck and hands, and unintentional,
this transformation will change
an adult to a child,
left to be forgetful and clumsy.

OLD AGE IS DIFFICULT,
it is a thief snatching your youth,
becoming the end of what once was.
This is when we start a new course in life,
with the destination an end of a cycle well lived.

THE ONLY THING left behind are the memories,
each one created in our walk through life,
So smile, be joyful, enjoy the little things in life,
love with all your heart and mind.

DANCE IN THE RAIN, shout out in laughter,
shed tears of pain and joy,
share freely, be kind to others,
because old age will

take you with no warning.

Permanent, no appointment made,
    destination unknown,
    any time, anywhere.
    No mercy.

YOUR APPROVAL

*D*o not give me reasons
        or motives to change.
Accept me as I am,
with my highs and lows.

ACCEPT MY PAST that has left
    foot prints in me, paths,
    love my defects.

COME CLOSER, don't walk away,
    I'm giving you what I am
    With all my madness,
    nonsense and endless stories.

ACCEPT ME WITH your open arms
    and learn to love me.
    And remember that we all have faults,

Do not judge mine.

ACCEPT ME WITH my achievements
and losses, with my open wounds.
Prove what you say and do not
let your words blow away.

ACCEPT ME AS I AM,
that my heart was made to love you.
Despite the good and bad events,
I am what I am.

MY SOUL, heart, and mind
accept you for who you are.

I JUST WANT YOUR APPROVAL, let me in.

HATEFUL WORLD

I was walking over the big blue world,
the mountains so majestic,
the blue ocean surrounding me.

I SAW A WORLD DYING,
devoid of love,
peace, and respect.

THE WORLD I saw was suffering,
leaving a red stain over
the cold big green landscape.

THE CAVIAR and champagne
flowed beside a hungry child
without food or shelter.

THE WEALTHY MASSES were throwing
  crumbs on the ground,
  to feed the elderly, the young,
  and homeless crowds.

SICKNESS AND HUNGER are everyday
  reminders...war, injustice, hate...
  the stereotypical garbage polluting
  our beautiful blue world.

  Humanity is dying slowly,
  stifled and besmirched is the true
  essence of our blue world.
  Why can't we get along in this world?

THE WORLD IS AS QUICKSAND,
  falling into the depths of
  sorrow and shame.

I CRY with pouring tears down my face
  as I look at all this beauty going to waste.
  I scream loudly, for my voice
  is becoming mute,
  because no one is listening.

MY HEAD HANGS LOW,
  because my strength
  has left me,
  with no hope in the future.

SARAH WILSON

I BECAME BLIND AND SPEECHLESS,
    unable to find freedom to
    choose, imprisoned with no escape.

I WILL NEVER BE FREE,
    for the hate is suffocating
    our hearts and our minds.

I FORGOT the meaning of tolerance
    and kindness, for everyone has
    lost their natural spirit.

WE ARE all afraid of change,
    but without it we lose the
    opportunity to have
    peace and happiness.

MY MEMORIES CAN'T FORGET
    the thick fog, as darkness
    covering our desolate hearts.

CAN we do something to
    end this misery?
    Lets get together and
    love one another.

WE ARE ALL THE SAME,
    longing to be united,

everything is possible
if we share our heart and mind.

WE CAN CHANGE the world
and make it wondrous,
the possibilities are endless…

THE DARKNESS IN MY ROOM

*I*n the darkness of my room
there are memories of a love
that was and is no longer

THE VAGUE NOSTALGIAS of lips
that existed and are no longer
The dim figure of a warm body
that was warm, but is now
covered with a blanket of ice

OH, ungrateful darkness,
why must you bring so many
unwanted memories?

AND LODGE them in my empty
pillow without mercy...
Oh darkness, I do not want

to be your slave once more.

WHY DO you have to raise
the skeleton of a dead love
that could not be?

OH DARKNESS, why must you
bring back the records of spells,
whispers of kisses and caresses?
Making the night an eternal honeymoon.

OH INCLEMENT DARKNESS,
let me cry and make a river of
this room without him.

I HATE YOU

I hate that I love you,
           and I hate that you don't
love me the same.
I hate that I want you so badly
and you don't even know my name.

I HATE my heart because it only
    wants to beat for you,
    but your heart is already beating
    for someone else.

I HATE my lips because they only
    want to kiss yours
    you don't even recognize them
    when they smile back at you longingly.

I HATE that my existence lingers,

just to feel your frozen
breath come my way.

I HATE that in my world,
    you are the reason I wake up
    every morning.

YOU DON'T EVEN NOTICE who I am,
    for you are occupied with
    someone else's advances.

I HATE that I don't give my heart
    the opportunity to love
    someone else and enjoy their glances.

I HATE that my eyes saw you
    that day and that my heart felt that way.
    I hate that I am dying slowly,
    and to survive would be the last
    thing I would want forever.

I NEVER THOUGHT LOVING
    and loathing someone
    could be so painful and foolish.

I CRAVE YOU

I crave you like the shore craves
     the waves, pounding hard
and parting slowly against the warm sand.

I CRAVE you more than nature
    needs the rain, you are more
    than just a void to me, lasting lust.

I CRAVE you because your lips
    tasted mine, and that is now
    the only thing that quenches my thirst.

I CRAVE you for fear that I may
    starve to death without feeling
    your warmth inside of me.

I HAVE LOVED BEFORE, but I never
 felt such a burning inside,
 lasting for hours, making me alive again.

I CRAVE you like a desert craves
 dewdrops on the parched ground.
 As he places his hands so delicately
 on each side of my body,
 the room disappears
 in the blink of an eye,
 and the blaze takes over.

I CRAVE you because when we
 are together, our bodies
 are intertwined as one,
 like a beautiful piece of art.

I CRAVE you like an alcoholic
 needs his drink, drinking from
 a bottomless glass.
 I crave you without shame,
 utterly addicted to you.

I LOVE YOU

I love you

Is all I want to say

I NEED you

ALWAYS WITH ME

I WANT you

LIKE NO ONE else will

IN THE MORNING

I love the way you tease me
        in the morning
When you are in control
and I'm gasping for air

How you make my stomach
    skip in a delightful way.
    You make my pulse race
    while enjoying each delicious thrill

I love the taste of you,
    the bitter delight of your sweat.
    I enjoy the way your tongue
    gently teases mine

As your fingertips trapped me
    in the warmth of your embrace, .

I surrender to his wildfire of
delicious pleasure.

As I GASP for breath in this blazing path,
  my legs buckle,
  grinding and molding to
  his shape, tangled in the covers.

His NAKED SKIN is a lullaby in the morning...

BE YOUR WIFE

I long to be the woman
            of your dreams.
the one you choose to be
your companion and holder of
innermost thoughts.
The only woman who says
goodnight to you in your bed.

I WANT to be the one who gazes
        into your eyes every morning
        upon awakening.
        The one whom you sigh for
        each time you dream,
         and share the moonlight
        each night by your side
        with loving embraces.

WHEN OUR EYES meet at a glance,

you cannot hide what is felt with blushes.
Let me be the one who satisfies
your desires completely.

I WILL BE the woman you trust
and share your deepest secrets with.
The one whom you call
friend, lover and wife.

FOR WITH THIS love you could
prolong your existence eternally
As time passes, the truthfulness
of her love is reflected in her smile.

To be your wife will be my only
wish, to create new stories
with you for a lifetime.
Come with me and stand
together under this threshold,
with all its brilliant lights.
And celebrate our union tonight,
and every night, as one.

MY MOTHER

I call you today my best friend,
my teacher, my rock.
With you I've shared my thoughts,
my dreams and secrets without fear.

You've always held my hand tightly,
anytime, anywhere, never letting go.
The way you brushed my hair and
tucked me in each night made me
confident in our love.

You are sweet and gentle,
softly speaking love in the
wisdom of your words.

Never have you let me down,
you have been my guiding light,

always by my side in the darkness.

YOU ARE UNIQUE,
no one compares to you,
you are my muse,
I wish to be you completely.

THE BOND we have is unbreakable,
attached from the womb
and forever in your heart.

I AM proud to be your daughter, Mom.
I am a piece of you forever.

SELFISH

I do not want to share your
love and your body
I do not desire to share
the taste of your lips and
your tender kisses

I DO NOT WANT to share your
dark blue eyes because I
wish to see myself in them.

I WANT to be your number one,
your best and only choice,
the only one…

TO BE the light that guides you
at night, the one who walks
with you in darkness

I WANT to be the sunlight,
   reflected in your face,
   every morning of each day

I DECLINE to make appointments
   to love you and make you mine
   I want to be yours,
   feeling you inside me until
   the end of our lives

I WISH NOT to share your past,
   because I want to be your
   today, your future

I WANT you for myself only,
   to be selfish and make you all mine
   I am not crazy, my mind is
   still with me, I just wish
   to be yours exclusively

YOU ARE the reason I live,
   my purpose in life, my goal,
   my everything.

GRIEVING HEART

*T*here is so much emptiness
        around our home,
so many beautiful memories
and hopes we've shared.

As I walk in every room,
    I feel your body lingering in every
    corner and wall, and I only close
    my eyes to see you standing there,
    smiling at me.

I cry out in disbelief,
    for I know you are not coming
    back to me, gone forever.

My anger blazes because we fought
    with all our strength, power

and energy, and we lost.

I REFUSE to believe that sickness is
stronger than our love and devotion,
but sadly it has won and taken
everything from you.

I CAN'T DESCRIBE the pain in my heart,
my soul is empty and my hope is gone.
If I could go back in time,
I would not change a thing
about our life together.

YOU CHANGED me and made me
a better person, and next to you
I learned the beauty of love
and the true meaning of love,
friendship, and passion.

I MISS YOU SO MUCH,
I need your kisses to survive,
my sense of living is no longer
the same without you.

AT NIGHT, I can see you in my dreams,
I can feel you breathing next to me.
You forgot to tell me how to survive
without you, I miss you my love.

I WILL SEE YOU, my love,
    when my time comes,
    be patient and wait for me.
    We will be together again in
    the land that our love has created,
    endless and eternal.

THE PERFECT MEDICINE

*Y*ou are the perfect medicine
that my body needs to survive
The love you give is the perfect
dose to fight all my illnesses.

YOUR KISSES ARE the fuel
that makes my heart beat faster.
A smile from you makes my
physical pain go away.

YOU RUSH THROUGH MY VEINS.
If I need oxygen, it is only your kiss
that I need to breathe in.

YOUR BEAUTIFUL EYES are the
magnifying glass that I need
to see into our world.

With each embrace of your arms,
I feel the warmth of your body.

THE LOVE you share with me
   is the best cure I need,
   the healing from your touch.

YOU QUENCH MY THIRST COMPLETELY.
   You satiate me like
   torrential waters hydrating my skin.
   You are my medicine,
   the perfect cure for my sickness,
   my condition, "being in love."

MY DEAR FRIEND

My dear friend, thank you
for always being there for me
when my days were full of darkness,
sorrow, worries, and tears.

YOU BRING HAPPINESS, joy, and huge
smiles to my heart after each rainy day.
I choose you to be my confidante
and my guide to walk with me along
the uneven path of life.

WE DON'T NEED to communicate every day,
for I am certain that I am in
your heart and thoughts.

WE HAD CRIED and laughed together,
no matter how serious or silly,

for we are connected as one.

YOU LISTEN best when my soul is crying ,
   you are there, in the silence to comfort me.
   We can be miles away, and I have
   confidence your heart and mind are beating to the
same song.

FOR YOU ARE MY COMPLEMENT,
   my other half,
   my partner in crime.

WITH ONE LOOK we both know
   everything is going to be fine.
   The days when you are absent,
   I miss all I could share with you.

MY HAPPIEST ACHIEVEMENTS
   and joyful days have seen
   your smile as well.

YOU ARE ONE IN A BILLION,
   the brightest star in a dark sky,
   the brilliance of a beautiful sunset.

I AM BLESSED to have you in my life,
   my friend, for it is easier to find a
   diamond on the street

than to find a friend like you
with open arms, a fearless heart

THAT IS WHO YOU ARE,
    and who I wish to be for you
    My dear friend, thank you for
    existing and making my life complete.

SCAR TISSUE

*S*adly you have become a
      permanent scar in my life.
I thought it was enough to see
the physical scars as a constant
reminder of my sadness.

BUT HOW MISGUIDED I have been
   all these years, you have
   scarred me endlessly

HOW LONELY A LIFE CAN BE,
   a virgin body trapped in a
   bubble, overprotected for no reason.

I'M SAD, I continue scared,
   petrified and anxious from
   all your volcanic reactions now

ALTHOUGH THE MEMORIES of you
    have become scar tissue,
    the pain is still as tender as the
    wound when it was freshly stabbed.

EVEN THOUGH THE times we had
    were good, darkness seems to
    cover the light so it cannot shine through.

MY SCARS HAVE BECOME
    more evident with the passing of time.
    Don't ask me why I behave and act
    this way, so tough, so callous.

MY BIGGEST SCAR has a
    name engraved, tucked within me....
    Your name...

MY BLIND EYES

*M*y blind eyes
        Why do you look so sad?
your eyes have many dry tears

WHY DON'T you see the way
    I see your life and mine?
    Why is so hard for you to feel
    the warm blood that runs
    through your veins?

WHY HAVE you refused to live
    day-by-day, and only revive the past?
    You have so much comfort and
    love in your surroundings,
    and you can't see it?

MY EYES ARE BLIND,

but I wish for you to see what I see
Wake up, my dear!
Look around you,
you have many wonders

I SEE it very clear and very shiny
every day near you
You have the freedom that
I wish to have some day

YOU HAVE endless possibilities
and three angels looking over you
Life is ironic, you can't see
those marvelous things in your life,
but I do…

I WOULD LOVE to lend you
my blind eyes for one day
Because through them,
you will see what I see...

TANGLE OF LOVE

I love the way you pull
my hair and my tender lips
close to your mouth
I can't get enough of your
wild movements in a crazy dance
with our tongues

MY BODY SURRENDERS to your call...
wanting you more and more
You and me becoming one,
molding to our shapes, fitting perfectly

OUR NAKED BODIES embracing in a
wild tangle of love
What a wonderful giddy skip
in my stomach and my body trembles

IT'S A DELICIOUS THRILL,
    feeling the stubbles in my skin,
    scratching me softly

I TASTE him and my fingertips
    travel gently, touching his manhood,
    sensations surrounding my body,
    gasping for air,
    ending in ecstasy.

TYRANT

I don't know why I even
        think of you,
  I do not understand why,
  if I'm always in pain.

My pathetic heart plays this game
    over and over with no end.
    I thought the shadows you left
    in your wake, were gone with your body.

But my heart is naive and blinded
    by the memories you left behind.
    My senses are confused,
    as my heart bleeds for you.
    I trusted my heart,
    but your love was never sincere,
    this painful truth I now know.

AS YOU PRETENDED TO PERFECTION,
    my heart and body believed you.
    I am no longer afraid to face the truth,
    to tell you what you really are.

YOU ARE A TYRANT,
    you have no decency,
    no heart, no soul

THE WORD MAN is too big for you.
    You do not care to understand
    the significance of love,
    your interior is sullen, empty, and dark.
    Many say time will heal my wounds,
    but my heart has many scars
    that have not healed.

NEITHER TIME nor distance
    will make my heart recover.
    You left me with a heart full of cuts,
    constantly open for the memories
    My body trembles when passing
    through the places that were once
    ours, and your scent again is
    revived with the air I breathe.

HOW INFAMOUS LIFE CAN BE!
    Being stepped on by someone,
    without even knowing it was a "mirage."

A UNIQUE GENTLEMAN

I like to observe you in detail
every time we are together,
you are peculiar indeed, a unique soul.

You slowly walk, thoughtfully,
as if the weight of the world were
on your shoulders, the weight
increasing with the passing of time,
full of stories and anecdotes told by you.

But some memories that you keep close and
locked, so raw and private, that rarely make
their way in conversation, only to be revealed
by you at the appropriate time,
reminding me how special you are to me.

You are such a unique character

as you become a storyteller,
stories that are so intimate,
which brings me happiness
as I listen to each detail.

So UNIQUE ARE YOUR WORDS,
that you make me imagine these
stories as fantastic, adventures
which have undoubtedly been
experienced by you, but I feel
as if I have been there too.

YOUR SHOULDERS ARE tired and
your slender legs have roads
you have walked long and winding,
full of illustrated characters,
who were with you as mirrors
reflecting busy lives.

I WANT to hear your fears, desires,
loves unfinished and unfulfilled dreams.
I want you to share with me
the happiest and saddest moments
of your life, I want to learn from you.

EACH LESSON LEAVING footprints
in my mind and heart, as they
have made for you and have molded
you into who you are today,

a unique gentleman in the book of your life.

YOU ARE a novel I want to read
    from beginning to end,
    filling myself with your knowledge,
    I respect you and love you

AND ALTHOUGH WE have in our history
    dark moments and tears,
    I now understand the "why's"
    of many situations in the past.
    Love sometimes covers over
    unnecessary pain and makes you blind.

ONLY WITH MISTAKES made and years
    passing by, do we start to be taught
    how to understand life,
    and teach others how to love.

YOU ARE GOING AWAY SOON,
    but I ask you to say your farewell
    very slowly. I want every minute
    to become an hour, and every hour
    a day, to have the pleasure of sharing

MY LIFE WITH YOUR LIFE, by your side.
    Even though we are not face to face,
    your words on the telephone are alive.

I want those phrases carefully
carved in my heart, encumbering
all that your voice represents,
to form a chain around my neck
as it touches my heart.

ABOUT THE AUTHOR

Sarah, or Angie as her friends call her "Saranyelina Wilson," is originally from Bogota Colombia and has lived in Boston, Massachusetts for the last 20 years with her loving husband and sweet chihuahua, Nacho.

She had always aspired to pursue journalism in some way, but at the age of twenty-five she suffered a brain aneurysm and massive stroke, which caused her to lose verbal and physical function temporarily on her left side.

She is an AVM (Arteriovenous malformation) survivor, skin cancer survivor, and legally blind. After experiencing so many life changing events, she decided to write a small collection of poetry to express the words she has held in her heart and soul all these years.

The way she feels and sees the world has changed over the years dramatically, but her views on life, love, friendship, sadness, and loss, have made her a new and improved version of the woman she always wanted to be.

Connect with Sarah online:
www.sarahwilsonbooks.wordpress.com

f

Made in United States
Orlando, FL
22 October 2024

53000911R00041